First World War
and Army of Occupation
War Diary
France, Belgium and Germany

GUARDS DIVISION
1 Guards Brigade
Headquarters
1 April 1917 - 30 April 1917

WO95/1213/7

The Naval & Military Press Ltd
www.nmarchive.com
Published in association with The National Archives

Published by

The Naval & Military Press Ltd

Unit 10 Ridgewood Industrial Park,

Uckfield, East Sussex,

TN22 5QE England

Tel: +44 (0) 1825 749494

www.naval-military-press.com

www.nmarchive.com

This diary has been reprinted in facsimile from the original. Any imperfections are inevitably reproduced and the quality may fall short of modern type and cartographic standards.

© **Crown Copyright**
Images reproduced by permission of The National Archives, London, England, 2015.

Contents

Document type	Place/Title	Date From	Date To
Heading	WO95/1213 April 1917		
War Diary	Arrow Head Copse	01/04/1917	16/04/1917
War Diary	Arrow Head C??? to Bronfay Camp 15.	17/04/1917	17/04/1917
War Diary	Bronfay Farm Camp 15.	18/04/1917	30/04/1917
Operation(al) Order(s)	1st Guards Brigade Order No. 110.	01/04/1917	01/04/1917
Miscellaneous	Appendix "A"		
Operation(al) Order(s)	1st Guards Brigade Order No. 119	05/04/1917	05/04/1917
Operation(al) Order(s)	1st Guards Brigade Order No. 120.	06/04/1917	06/04/1917
Operation(al) Order(s)	1st Guards Brigade Order No. 120.	14/04/1917	14/04/1917
Miscellaneous	March Table.		
Miscellaneous	Reference 1st Guards Brigade Order No. 120.	14/04/1917	14/04/1917
Operation(al) Order(s)	1st Guards Brigade Order No. 121.	30/04/1917	30/04/1917

5095
12123
April 1913

WAR DIARY or INTELLIGENCE SUMMARY

Army Form C. 2118

Headquarters 1st Guards Brigade

April 1917

Place	Date	Hour	Summary of Events and Information	Remarks and references to Appendices
ARROW HEAD COPSE	1st April		Very bad weather with high wind. Brigadier went to a service in Y.M.C.A. hut at MONTAUBAN. After service interviewed two companies 3rd C.G. Visited Works B.C. and Gds Entrenching Batt. after lunch walked to 2nd C.G. at MAUREPAS.	AH 232
ARROW HEAD COPSE	2nd		Hard frost during night. Morning fine but very cold and overcast with high wind. In afternoon Brigadier visited Capt. 2/5 Rl/Cy to arrange vacation of Fatigues. Tuesdays. Found men on fatigues changing for work.	
ARROW HEAD COPSE	3rd		Fine day. Very cold during the morning but milder in the afternoon. Brigadier in morning rode to see LES BOEUFS — LE TRANSLOY road with C.R.E. 33rd after luncheon visited M.G. Coys 2nd C.G. moved down MAUREPAS to reserve.	
ARROW HEAD COPSE	4th		Heavy snow all morning. In afternoon Brigadier visited the Brussels Q.H.Q. and then U.S.A. had decided to be on warring the Brigadier visited 1st C.G. in new camp at GINCHY, many of H.Q. and 3rd C.G. helped to dig in to the snow.	AH 337
ARROW HEAD COPSE	5th		Brigadier visited Battalions working on ballast pit extension line L.F. to Officers Gds in new camp. Reached LE TRANSLOY. In aft. at 4 pm Brigadier visited 3rd C.G. in new head. Going on new to Y.E. and old C.F. in LE TRANSLOY. Road and snow all day.	
ARROW HEAD COPSE	6th		Brigadier visited during the morning fatigue parties working on the railway, and visited the camps of 3rd & 2nd C.G. who with 1st C.G. on road to LE TRANSLOY on this date, till midday, afterwards and various days he during the afternoon turned out with heavy rain, in the evening visited 2nd C.G.	AH 352

WAR DIARY or INTELLIGENCE SUMMARY

Army Form C. 2118

Place	Date	Hour	Summary of Events and Information	Remarks and references to Appendices
ARROW HEAD COPSE	7th		Snow and frost in early morning. Strong wind and some rain fell into a thin slush in the afternoon. Brigadier visited the troops [?] on railway; also visited sundry adv. H. Btty. The 2nd GG and 2nd C.G. moved this morning. 3rd G. Brigade new name LE TRANSLOY.	
ARROW HEAD COPSE	8th		Easter Day. A very fine warm day. All battalion main camps. Yachting day which gave us [?] absence to G.O.C. He was unable to put in to Bn. Hqrs 10.0. Brigadier did not go out till afternoon when he visited sundry [?] Army Column. Major Prance visited Brigade HQrs during afternoon.	
ARROW HEAD COPSE	9th		Brigadier went up to LE TRANSLOY and visited 2nd G.G. in [?] down the new trench to [?] see working parties. Much work has been done. Cold day with high wind and heavy showers.	
"	10th		Brigadier visited all working parties.	
"	11th		Brigadier together with G.S.O.1 & 4th Army inspected all work in progress on the broad gauge Railway. Much progress had been made but there were still complaints from all units that more men were required for the work than were demanded by R.E.	
"	12th		All working parties on railways again visited by Brigadier.	
"	13th	9pm	Orders received from Div for Bde to move to BILLON or BRONFAY camps for training.	

Army Form C. 2118

WAR DIARY
or
INTELLIGENCE SUMMARY
(Erase heading not required.)

Instructions regarding War Diaries and Intelligence Summaries are contained in F.S. Regs., Part II. and the Staff Manual respectively. Title Pages will be prepared in manuscript.

Place	Date	Hour	Summary of Events and Information	Remarks and references to Appendices
ARROW HEAD COPSE	April 14.	8 am	1st Bde Bde Order 120 issued to units	APP. 355
	April 15		2nd Coldstream & 1st Irish Gds - 1st Gds Bde 2.F.Coy & T.M.Bty. marched to BRONFAY Farm Camp 15. The weather was bad & it was a long march especially for troops that had not done a march for several months but it was well carried out. The march discipline & transport called for some attention.	
	April 16.		2nd Gren Gds & 3rd Coldstream Gds continued work on the ROCQUIGNY Railway under 295 Coy R.E. The LES BOEUFS - LE TRANSLOY road was opened & & made passable for horse drawn transport.	
ARROW HEAD (Copse to) BRONFAY Camp 15.	April 17		Bde H.Q. 2nd Gren Gds & 3rd Coldstream Gds moved in very stormy weather to BRONFAY Farm Camp.	

WAR DIARY
or
INTELLIGENCE SUMMARY

Army Form C. 2118

Place	Date	Hour	Summary of Events and Information	Remarks and references to Appendices
BRONFAY Farm Camp 15.	April 12th to 28th		The whole of this period was devoted to platoon training - a programme on the following lines was carried out daily by every unit of the Bde. 7 am — Run. 8.30 am to 9.30 am Steady drill — a battalion parade — men to attend thy parade — all employed 10 am to 12.15 pm } Platoon training — Musketry - bayonet fighting - Training of Specialists. 2 pm to 3 pm } Great stress was laid in the first part of this period of platoons as laid down in O.B. 1919 (Organisation of an Inf Bn?) correct. Emphasis was laid on the fact that on every parade sections should always fall in the same place - section commanders always with their own sections. Men were not to be taken away from platoons except by order of the platoon commander or when it was necessary to find a fatigue and must was to be detailed rather than a number of men. The first period of this training was devoted almost entirely to mushtry - bayonet fighting - bombing, & the training of each section in the weapon in which at specialised. The great difficulty to be contended with were (1) lack of instructors - section commanders in many cases not being sufficiently experienced to train their sections - specially in the case of Rifle grenade sections. (2) The difficulty of instilling into all ranks that the first weapon of every infantry man were the rifle & bayonet — the second weapon of the Coy, & that the weapon in which 3 sections in each platoon specialised were only special weapons to come	

WAR DIARY or INTELLIGENCE SUMMARY

Army Form C. 2118

Place	Date	Hour	Summary of Events and Information	Remarks and references to Appendices
	April 30th		after the rifle, bayonet & bomb in order of importance. Gradually all units worked up to tactical schemes & trench to trench attacks but each day one hour was always spent in steady drill & one hour in the training of specialists. During the hour when musketry training was going on rifle sections were split up & the men trained in some specialist weapon. The only course during this period was a Bde Bombing course for those men of bombing sections who had not been through a course. This course finished on April 25th & the Bde instructors were then lent to Bns as required by them for advanced training of bombing or rifle grenade sections. All Bombing sections were constituted as follows — 2 Squads each consisting of 1 N.C.O., 1 Bomber, 1 Carrier, 1 Bayonet man, 1 Rifle grenade man + their instructor consisted the Bde Signalling Officer. Every unit had it's own short range & there was a Rifle 200 3ft range allotted to units for dark daily. Areas were allotted. Lectures were given on Ultimate afternoons in Discipline, attack, Open warfare attack, Trench to trench attack, Kitchener's lectures all ranks on Bayonet fighting on April 30th	

Major Campbell D.S.O.

WAR DIARY or INTELLIGENCE SUMMARY

Army Form C. 2118

Place	Date	Hour	Summary of Events and Information	Remarks and references to Appendices
BRONFAY Farm Camp 15.	April 30th		On this date Company training started but at 10am orders were received to move two Battalions to ETRICOURT for work on FINS - ROCQUIGNY railway. Training started accordingly at 4pm accordingly 2nd Bn Coldstream & 1st Bn Irish Gds moved to MAUREPAS for the night. Platoons in for the final of the Platoon competition remained. 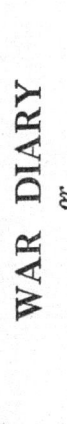 As did also signallers. In the morning the musketry part of the Platoon competition was fired. The shooting was at 200 yds range 5 rounds slow 5 rounds rapid (30 secs allowed) for all platoons an average of 13.5 (out of a possible 50) only being obtained. 1st Bn Coldstream Order No 121 issued during this period of training was fine & dry with the exception of the first two days. This facilitated training to a large extent

Signed [signature]
Brig General
Comdg 1st Guards Bde | left (camp) 356 |

S E C R E T.   Copy No. 11.

1st Guards Brigade Order No. 113.

1st April 1917.

1.   The following movement of Units will take place after work on April 3rd, to ensure closer supervision.

Unit.	From.	To.	Take over Camp and work from -
1/Irish Gds.	GONELEU.	MONTAUBAN.	2/Irish Gds.
2/Cold.Gds.	HAUDEPAS.	GUYNCY.	3/Gren.Gds.

2.   All details of relief will be arranged direct between Battalions concerned.

3.   Appendix "A" shows distribution and work of Units in the Brigade on April 4th.

        ACKNOWLEDGE.

                                F. Beaumont Nesbitt. Captain,
                                a/Brigade Major, 1st Guards Brigade.

Copy No.1 2nd Bn. Grenadier Guards.
        2 2nd Bn. Coldstream Guards.
        3 3rd Bn. Coldstream Guards.
        4 1st Bn. Irish Guards.
        5 2nd Guards Brigade.
        6 Guards Division.
        7 Staff Captain.
        8 Supply Officer.
        9 - 11 Retained.

APPENDIX "A".

Unit.	Location.	For.	Will receive orders from.
2nd Bn.Gren.Gds.	GINCHY.	LES BOEUFS - LE TRANSLOY Rd.	C.E.
3rd Bn.Cold.Gds.	GINCHY.	Broadgauge Railway.	89th Railway Coy. R.E.
2nd Bn.Cold.Gds.	MONTAUBAN.	B Coy's.LES BOEUFS - LE TRANSLOY Rd. S Coy's.Broadgauge Railway,LEUZE Wood.	C.E. 89th Railway Coy. R.E.
1st Bn.Irish Gds.	MONTAUBAN.	Broadgauge Railway.	89th Railway Coy. R.E.
M.G.Company & T.M.Battery.	LE TRANSLOY.	(SOUTH COPSE Douaville (LE TRANSLOY - LES BOEUFS Rd.	C. R. E.

SECRET.   Copy No. 10

1st Guards Brigade Order Number 119.

5th April 1917.

1. **MOVE.**
   The following movement of Units will take place tomorrow, 6th inst., :-
   3rd Bn. Coldstream Guards from Camp at MONTAUBAN to a Camp at O.31.b.5.3.
   1st Bn. Irish Guards from COMBLES to a Camp near SUCRERIE, N.24.d.3.6.

2. **HOUR of DEPARTURE.**
   The hour of departure is left at the discreation of Officers Commanding Battalions.

3. **FATIGUES.**
   No Corps fatigues will be found by the above mentioned Battalions on the day on which they move to their new Camps.

4. **TENTS.**
   75 Tents per Battalion will be sent under arrangements made by the Guards Division, to be at Road junction O.31.b.4.0. at 11-30 AM 6th inst.,
   Advanced parties will be detailed to meet these Tents, point out the positions of the new Camps and off-load the Tents.

5. **RATIONS.**
   Rations for the two Battalions will be sent by Decauville to COMBLES at an hour to be notified later and taken on from there in Limbers by the Battalions.

6. **WATER.**
   There is a Water Point at Road junction O.31.b.4.0.

7. **CAMP COMMANDANT.**
   Captain E. O. STEWART, Grenadier Guards, is appointed Camp Commandant, Guards Division Camps, LE TRANSLOY.

8. **1st LINE TRANSPORT.**
   1st Line Transport and Details need not move from their present billets, until Battalions have made arrangements to accommodate them in their new area.

9. **COMMUNICATION.**
   All communication with 1st Guards Brigade Headquarters will, until further notification, be through H.Q., Guards Division.

   ACKNOWLEDGE.

                                                    Captain,
                                    a/Brigade Major, 1st Guards Brigade.

Issued through Signals at 8-30 P.M.

          Copy No.1 3rd Bn. Coldstream Guards.
               2 1st Bn. Irish Guards.
               3 2nd Guards Brigade.
               4 Guards Division.
               5 Camp Commdt., LE TRANSLOY.
               6 Supply Officer.
               7 Staff Captain.
               8 Signals.
               9 - 11 Retained.

SECRET.

Copy No. 9.

1st Guards Brigade Order No.120.

April 6th, 1917.

1. **MOVE.**

    The following movement of Units will take place tomorrow, 7th inst., :-

    2nd Bn. Grenadier Guards from Camp at GINCHY to a Camp O.26.c.0.9.

    2nd Bn. Coldstream Guards from Camp at GINCHY to a Camp O.31.b.5.2.

2. **HOUR of DEPARTURE.**

    The hour of departure is left at the discretion of Officers Commanding Battalions.

3. **FATIGUES.**

    No Corps fatigues will be found by the above mentioned Battalions on the day on which they move to their new Camps.

4. **TENTS.**

    The Tents now in use at GINCHY Camps will be taken by the Battalions concerned to their new Camps.

5. **WAGGONS.**

    Ten waggons per Battalion will be available for moving tents and blankets.

6. **RATIONS.**

    Rations for the two Battalions will be sent by Decauville to COMBLES at an hour to be notified later, and taken on from there in Limbers by the Battalions.

7. **WATER.**

    There is a water point at Road Junction O.31.b.4.0.

8. **CAMP COMMANDANT.**

    Captain E.O. Stewart, Grenadier Guards, is appointed Camp Commandant, Guards Division Camp, LE TRANSLOY.

9. **1st LINE TRANSPORT.**

    1st Line Transport and Details need not move from their present billets, until Battalions have made arrangements to accommodate them in their new area.

10. **COMMUNICATION.**

    All communication with 1st Guards Brigade Headquarters will, until further notification, be through H.Q., Guards Division.

F. Beaumont Nesbitt
Captain,
a/Brigade Major, 1st Guards Brigade.

Copy No. 1 2nd Bn. Grenadier Guards.
2 2nd Bn. Coldstream Guards.
3 Guards Division.
4 Senior Supply Officer.
5 Staff Captain.
6 Camp Commdt., LE TRANSLOY.
7 Signals.
8-10 Retained.

S E C R E T.  Copy No. 14

1st Guards Brigade Order No. 120.

Ref.Map - ALBERT 1/40,000.   April 14th, 1917.

1. The 1st Guards Brigade will move to the BRONFAY or BILLON Farm Area in accordance with attached March Table.

2. Details as to provision of additional Transport, movement of Tents, and taking over of new Camps, will be issued later.

3. Details now with Works Battalion will rejoin their Units under Battalion arrangements on the day on which their Units move - unless otherwise desired by C. O's. in which case this Office must be informed.

4. 1st Line Transport will move in rear of Unit.

5. Billeting parties will report to the Staff Captain at the Camp which is being taken over at 10-30 a.m. on the date on which the move of their Unit takes place.

6. 1st Guards Brigade H.Q., will close at ARROW HEAD COPSE and open at BRONFAY Farm, Camp 15, at 2 p.m. on April 17th.

ACKNOWLEDGE.

Captain,
Brigade Major, 1st Guards Brigade.

Issued to Signals at 8 a.m.

Copy No. 1 2nd Bn. Grenadier Guards.   Copy No. 7 Guards Division.
         2 2nd Bn. Coldstream Guards.   8 1st Gds.Bde. Supply Officer.
         3 3rd Bn. Coldstream Guards.   9   "   "   Transport Offr.
         4 1st Bn. Irish Guards.   10   "   "   Signal Officer.
         5 Bde. Machine Gun Company.   11 Town Major, LE TRANSLOY.
         6 Bde. Trench Mortar Battery.   12 Staff Captain.
                                                13 - 15 Retained.
                                                16. 1st Gds Bde Works
                                                         Detachment

MARCH TABLE.

Date.	Unit.	From.	To.	Route.	Remarks.
April 15th.	2/Cold.Gds.	LE TRANSLOY.	BILLON or BROMFAY.	COMBLES - MAUREPAS - MARICOURT.	To start from Camp at 8-15 a.m.
	1/Irish Gds.	"	"	"	" " " " " 9-45 a.m.
	1st Gds.Bde. M.G.Coy. & T.M.Bty.	"	"	"	" " " " " 10-45 a.m.
April 17th.	2/Gren.Gds.	ROCQUIGNY.	"	"	" " " " " 9-30 a.m.
	3/Cold.Gds.	LE TRANSLOY.	"	"	" " " " " 8-15 a.m.
	1st Gds.Bde. Hd.Qrs.,	ARROW HEAD COPSE.	BROMFAY.	MARICOURT.	" " " " " 2 p.m.

Units will move by Coy's. at 500 yards interval between Coy's.
An interval of 500 yards will be maintained between every 4 transport vehicles.
After 2 hours marching there will be half-an-hours halt (1st Line Transport inclusive) during which haversack rations will be consumed.

S E C R E T.   Copy No. 14

Reference 1st Guards Brigade Order No.120.

Ref, Map - ALBERT 1/40,000.   April 14th, 1917.

1. **WAGGONS.**

Waggons will be detailed on the 15th inst., as under :-

		Blankets.	Tents.
2nd Bn. Coldstream Gds.)	To be found	4 waggons.	6 waggons.
1st Bn. Irish Guards.)	by D. A. C.	4 "	6 "
1st Gds.Bde. M.G.Coy.)	To be found by	3 "	2 "
and T.M.Battery.)	Divnl. Train.		

Waggons will report at DROMORE CORNER, O.31.b.4.0., at 6 a.m. Units will arrange to have guides to meet them.

2. **TENTS & MARQUEES.**

Units, except 2nd Bn. Grenadier Guards, will strike and pack their Tents, complete with pegs, on to the waggons detailed for the purpose.

All Tents will be returned, and a return of the numbers forwarded to this Office as soon as possible.

Tents will be taken to Guards Division Ordnance, HARICOURT.

The Camp of the 2nd Bn. Grenadier Guards will not be struck but will be handed over to the 2nd Bn. Irish Guards at 8 a.m. on 17th inst., and a return of the number of tents and marquees handed over forwarded to this Office.

3. **RATIONS.**

Rations for Units at BRONFAY will be sent by Decauville at an hour to be notified later.

4. **CAMPS.**

Billeting parties will report to the Staff Captain at the Town Majors Office, BRONFAY 15 at 10-30 a.m. on the date on which the move of a Unit takes place.

for Staff Captain, 1st Guards Brigade.

Copy No.1 2nd Bn. Grenadier Guards.   Copy No.8 1st Gds.Bde. Supply Officer.
      2 2nd Bn. Coldstream Guards.   9   "   "   Transport Offr.
      3 3rd Bn. Coldstream Guards.   10   "   "   Signal Officer.
      4 1st Bn. Irish Guards.   11 Town Major, LE TRANSLOY.
      5 Bde. Machine Gun Company.   12 1st Gds.Bde. Works Detachment.
      6 Bde. Trench Mortar Battery.   13 - 15 Retained.

SECRET.   Copy No. 12

(356)

1st Guards Brigade Order No. 121.

Ref Maps - ALBERT. 1/40,000.   April 30th, 1917.
           57 C.   1/40,000.

1.
   (a)   2nd Bn. Coldstream Guards and 1st Bn. Irish Guards will
         move from MAUREPAS tomorrow May 1st to Camps at ETRICOURT.

   (b)   Route.

         For Personnel - COMBLES - SAILLISEL - thence cross country
                         to MANANCOURT.

         For Transport - COMBLES - SAILLY SAILLISEL - ROCQUIGNY -
                         LE MESNIL - MANANCOURT.

   (c)   1st Bn. Irish Guards will clear Camp at MAUREPAS by 10-30 a.m.

         2nd Bn. Coldstream Guards will not move before 11 a.m.

   (d)   Intervals of 500 yards between Coy's. and every 4 vehicles
         will be maintained. Troops will march in file East of
         COMBLES.

2.   2nd Bn. Coldstream Guards and 1st Bn. Irish Guards will
   each detail following parties to ~~load and~~ off load tents :-

   ~~(a)~~ ~~1 N.C.O. and 5 O.R. to go to 15th Corps Ordnance at
         QUINCONCE just
         N.W. of PERONNE on May 1st to load 140 tents into 8
         lorries. These lorries will pick up the loading party
         at Level Crossing MAUREPAS RAVINE at 7 a.m. and party
         will proceed with lorries to QUINCONCE and on to ETRICOURT
         after loading up with tents.~~

   (b)   1 Officer 30 O.R. to be at ETRICOURT at 10-30 a.m. to off
         load 140 tents from QUINCONCE and pitch the Camp.

3.   2nd Bn. Coldstream Guards and 1st Bn. Irish Guards are each
   allotted 70 tents.

4.   A Staff Officer from Guards Division H.Q., will be at
   ETRICOURT at 10-30 a.m. to point out sites selected for Camps
   to Officers in charge of the parties mentioned in para 2 (b).

5.   The 4 G.S. Wagons now with 2nd Bn. Coldstream Guards and
   1st Bn. Irish Guards will move surplus kit of these Battalions
   tomorrow and remain with Battalions for night of May 1st/2nd
   returning to Guards Divisional Train on May 2nd.

(2)

6. Platoons remaining in Camp 15 for Platoon Competition will rejoin their Battalions on May 3rd under orders to be issued direct to Platoons concerned from this Office.

7. ~~2nd Bn. Coldstream Guards and 1st Bn. Irish Guards will wire what Transport is required to move surplus kit left in Camp 15, and if not required before May 3rd, transport will be demanded to move it on that date.~~

8. On arrival at ETRICOURT 2nd Bn. Coldstream Guards and 1st Bn. Irish Guards will be required for work on ROCQUIGNY - FINS Railway. Lt-Col. G.B.S. Follett, M.V.O., D.S.O., will co-ordinate all work of 2nd Bn. Coldstream Guards and 1st Bn. Irish Guards.

Work will start on May 2nd and work will be notified by R.C.E. 4th Army direct to Lt-Col. G.B.S. Follett.

ACKNOWLEDGE.

Captain,
Brigade Major, 1st Guards Brigade.

Issued at 6-30 p.m.

Copy No. 1 2nd Bn. Grenadier Guards.
2 2nd Bn. Coldstream Guards.
3 3rd Bn. Coldstream Guards.
4 1st Bn. Irish Guards.
5 Bde. Machine Gun Company.
6 Bde. Trench Mortar Battery.
7 Guards Division, "G".
8 Guards Division, "Q".
9 Brigade Supply Officer.
10 Staff Captain.
11 O.C., Signals.
12 - 15 Retained.

www.ingramcontent.com/pod-product-compliance
Lightning Source LLC
Chambersburg PA
CBHW081511160426
43193CB00014B/2652